The Old Hatfield Historic Trail

Mark Bolitho

Mark Bolitho

Hatfield 1818

Special thanks to Brian Lawrence who supported the project by sharing his historical research and supplying some of the text and historical photos that are included in this book.

HATFIELD FROM THE RAILWAY STATION.

Copyright © 2018 Mark Bolitho

All rights reserved.

ISBN-13: 978-1719347259
ISBN-10: 1719347255

INTRODUCTION

This book is intended to accompany you on a walk around the area we now call Old Hatfield. It highlights some buildings and stories that give an idea of the history of the town as it was.

The history of Hatfield can be traced back over a thousand years. Its first historical mention is 970 AD, when King Edgar gave land to the monks of Ely. The Domesday Book from 1086 records 'Hetfelle' as having a Parish Priest and 55 inhabitants. Nothing remains of this settlement, as buildings were replaced and recycled. The earliest parts of the Church of St Etheldreda date from the 13th century.

The monks managed the land for many years and in 1479 Cardinal Morton organized the construction of the Bishop's Palace. In 1538 the Manor of Hatfield became crown property and the land was acquired by Henry VIII. The house became a home for his children, including the young Queen Elizabeth.

In 1607 King James I traded Hatfield for another estate known as Theobalds, owned by Robert Cecil and located in the south of the County, in Cheshunt. Robert Cecil, and his family moved to Hatfield and set about dismantling the existing palace to build the Hatfield House that stands today.

In the 17th Century the main road between London and the North passed through Hatfield. The road ran up what is now Fore Street, and turned right outside what is now the gate house entrance to Hatfield Park. Hatfield's location on the main road brought steady growth and trade to the town and associated businesses grew up to support travellers resting overnight. The town had many inns, lodgings and a brewery.

Changes in transport technology led to the arrival of the mainline railway in 1850. At the same time the Great North Road, was rerouted to run parallel to the path of the new railway.

Changes in the road network and transportation technology have continued to effect the area. In 1927 the Barnet-by-Pass rerouted again taking traffic away from the original town. This road, the current A1, replaced the A1000 as the main route between London and the North.

Although the railway had initially brought growth and prosperity, the changes to roads diverted traffic that had previously passed through. Travellers between London and the North were less likely to stop in Hatfield. Businesses and Inns that had previously supported coach travellers, changed and modernized to become garages for motor cars. More efficient transport methods also meant that travellers no longer required an overnight stay.

Local changes also took place. In the late 1960s plans were drawn up to reroute the A1000 and develop Salisbury Square into a pedestrianized area. The town previously known as Hatfield became known as Old Hatfield. This resulted in many of the older buildings being demolished to make way for the new road.

Following a charrette, hosted by the current Lord Salisbury at Hatfield House in 2008, new plans have been put forward to redevelop Salisbury square again.

Although the area that is now called Old Hatfield has changed over the years, it still carries echoes of its history. This walking trail will take you on a journey through the town of today and highlight some stories from its past.

Opposite page: The Hatfield Trail drawn by James Wilding

3

HISTORY AND TIMELINE

The history of Hatfield dates back many hundreds of years. There is no archaeological evidence of a Roman settlement despite the towns proximity to Verulamium (St. Albans) and the baths at Welwyn. The following is a list of significant events in the History of Hatfield.

970 AD	Land is given to the Abbotts of Ely by King Edgar, it became Bishop's Hatfield.
1086	Hetfelle is listed in the Domesday Book. Hatfield's entry shows a small settlement with two watermills and 55 people.
1479	Cardinal Morton builds the Old Palace.
1538	King Henry VIII takes over the bishop's palace.
1558	Queen Elizabeth I received the news of her accession to the throne while sitting an Oak tree in Hatfield Park.
1608	James I, trades his palace at Hatfield for Theobalds, the Cecil family estate in Hertfordshire. Robert Cecil demolished most of the Old Palace and used the bricks to build the Hatfield House.
1611	Hatfield House completed.
1837	Queen Victoria ascends the throne.
1848	William Lamb dies and is buried in St. Etheldreda's. He served two terms as Prime Minister of Great Britain.
1850	Opening of the Great Northern Railway (GNR) from London to York (with Hatfield as one of the original stops). The Great North Road is re routed to run parallel to the railway.
1885	Robert Arthur Talbot Gascoyne-Cecil, 3rd Marquess of Salisbury, became Prime Minister of Great Britain.
1903	Robert Arthur Talbot Gascoyne-Cecil, dies and is buried at St. Etheldreda's church.
1914-1918	World War I. Tests of the first tank were carried out in Hatfield Park.

1920	Ebenezer Howard builds Welwyn Garden City
1927	The Barnet by pass opens re routing traffic away from the Great North Road.
1928	de Havilland Aeronautical Technical School opens. It eventually becomes the Hatfield Polytechnic and is now the University of Hertfordshire.
1934	The de Havilland Aircraft Company opened its new factory at Hatfield.
1939-1945	World War II
1948	14th June 1948 Hatfield designated as a New Town
1968	Salisbury square pedestrianised and A1000 road rerouted.
1970	Marychurch opens in Old Hatfield
1986	Hatfield Tunnel carrying the A1M opened. Since then vehicles pass under the town rather than through it, as they had done for centuries previously.
1993	Aircraft manufacturing ends at Hatfield
2000	17 October 2000 – Hatfield train crash resulted in the deaths of four passengers.
2008	Robert Cecil, 7th Marquess of Salisbury, announced plans to redevelop Old Hatfield.
2011	Hatfield House celebrated its 400th anniversary. New additions included a sundial in the West Garden and a fountain in the stable yard.
2015	A new Hatfield Station opens

Mark Bolitho

THE HATFIELD TRAIL

Locations in Old Hatfield on the walking trail

1) Hatfield Station
2) The Entrance to Hatfield House
3) The Great Northern
4) Salisbury Square
5) Marychurch
6) The Burgess Memorial
7) The Salisbury Restaurant and former town jail
8) Church Street
9) Jacobs Ladder
10) St. Audrey's
11) No. 5 Church Street
12) St Ethedreda's Church Hall
13) Church Cottage
14) St Etheldreda's church
15) Inside St Etheldreda's church
16) The Salisbury burial ground
17) The real tennis court
18) The Old Palace
19) Stable Yard
20) The old Salisbury Arms
21) East India House
22) Fore Street
23) The Eight Bells
24) Chequers Inn
25) Site of Park Street Chapel
26) The Horse and Groom
27) Arm and Sword Lane
28) Hill House
29) Hatfield Viaduct
30) Junction of Park Street. and Old Hertford Road
31) The Red Lion
32) North Place
33) Hatfield Social Club
34) Marquis House
35) The Hatfield War Memorial

Appendix

A) Hatfield Park War Cemetery
B) Hatfield Rail Crash Memorial
C) Mill Green Village and Museum

The numbered locations on the map opposite refer to the locations above. More detailed information can be found in each section of the book. The locations marked by letters refer to other place of interest in the appendix.

- Local History Information boards
- Trail sites
- Additional locations

The Red Lion

Old Hertford Road

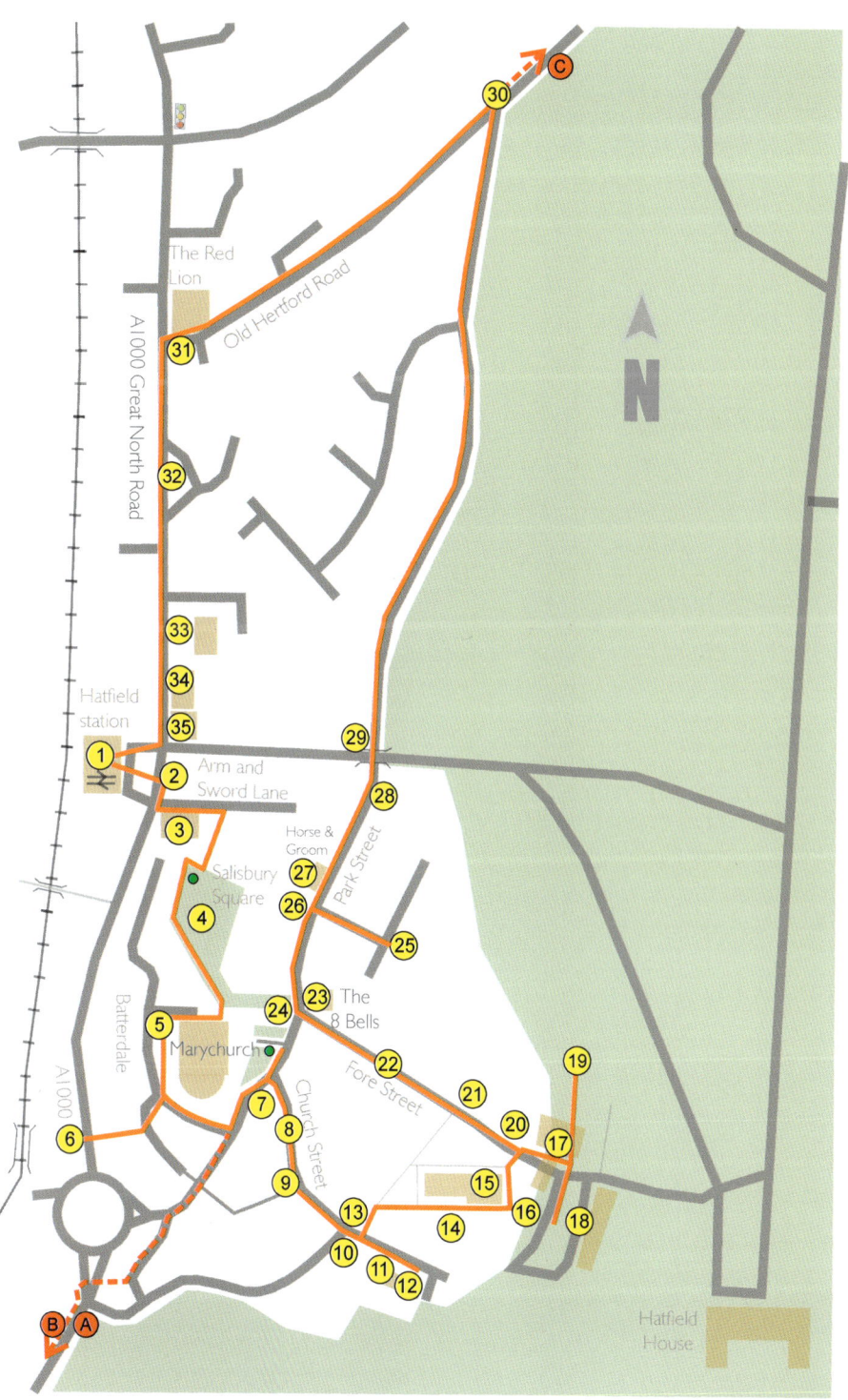

A1000 Great North Road

Hatfield station

Arm and Sword Lane

Horse & Groom

Salisbury Square

Park Street

The 8 Bells

Marychurch

Batterdale

A1000

Church Street

Fore Street

Hatfield House

7

(1) HATFIELD STATION

The railway came to Hatfield in 1850 during the reign of Queen Victoria.

The first Hatfield station, built in 1850, formed part of the Great North Railway (GNR). This railway ran between London and York, and Hatfield became an important stop on this route. As the railways expanded Hatfield became an interchange station with branch lines connecting to St Albans (from 1868) and Dunstable.

The original station had covered platforms with several waiting rooms, including one for the exclusive use of Lord Salisbury and his guests. The station platforms are offset, and do not face each other. The reasons for this are unclear, but may be due to other features of the original station.

The 1950s and 60s saw a decline in railways and the contraction of the network lead to the closure of these connecting routes. The Hatfield and St Albans Railway closed to in 1951 and the route to Dunstable North closed in 1965 as part of the Beeching network reforms. The route of the St. Albans line is now a cycle and pedestrian path called the Alban way.

The station has been re-developed many times. The original wooden structures have been replaced and rebuilt. However, the offset platforms remain in their original positions. In 2015 a new station was opened along with retail units and a multi-storey car park.

Immediately opposite Hatfield station is a statue of Lord Salisbury and the gates of Hatfield House.

Hatfield Station around 1920

(2) THE ENTRANCE TO HATFIELD HOUSE

The Entrance to Hatfield House with a statue of former Prime Minister Lord Salisbury (1830 -1903).

The arrival of the station was an important development for the town. The railway formed a new fast and efficient connection to London. In response a new entrance to Hatfield House was constructed. A viaduct was constructed along with a gatehouse and iron gates. This enabled direct access from the station to the house. This is the entrance that now faces the station.

The gates and gatehouse were commissioned in 1878 by the 3rd Marquess of Salisbury and constructed by E W Turner of St Albans. The gate posts are formed from four white stone pillars supporting statues of lions holding shields. The gates themselves are cast-iron.

In 1906 a statue of Lord Salisbury was commissioned to sit opposite the station and greet rail travelers. To accommodate this the original gates were moved back several yards.

The Salisbury Statue was designed and sculpted by George Frampton and unveiled by the Earl of Clarendon on 20 October 1906.

The statue commemorates the 3rd Marquess of Salisbury (1830 - 1903). Lord Salisbury held office for three terms as Prime Minister to Queen Victoria, (23 June 1885 to 28 January 1886), (25 July 1886 to 11 August 1892) and (25 June 1895 to 11 July 1902). He is buried in St. Etheldreda's church.

(3) THE GREAT NORTHERN

The Great Northern opened with the coming of the railway in 1850.

The Inn opposite the station took the name the Great Northern Inn, emphasising its proximity to the railway. The building on the current site dates from around 1900.

The Great Northern has had many names over the years, including the Douro Arms and more recently the Hatfield Arms. It is one of four public houses in Old Hatfield to have withstood the extensive re-development of the town over the years.

The Great Northern around 1900. The buildings on either side are now demolished.

Soldiers march past the Great Northern and the Hatfield Cinema in 1918

(4) SALISBURY SQUARE

Salisbury Square - Former brewery site redeveloped in the 1960s to become a pedestrianised square.

The current Salisbury Square was constructed in the 1960s as a pedestrianised area at the heart of the Old Hatfield development created by the re-routing of the A1000. It has undergone many changes over the years.

The square was the site of a brewery since at least the 17th century. The first brewery was built by the Searancke family and later acquired by the Pryor family in the 1830s. The brewery continued to prosper under the name Pryor Reid & Co until the end of the First World War when the brewery was sold to Benskins of Watford.

In the north corner of the square is a plaque with a map of Hatfield and historical notes. Next door is the town noticeboard.

At the South side of the square we can find Marychurch.

The Pryor Reid Brewery once stood on Brewery Hill on what is now Salisbury Square.

The view of St Etheldreda's from the Great North Road. The buildings on the right now form one side of the Salisbury Square.

(5) MARYCHURCH

Marychurch. The Roman Catholic church, built in 1970 is a Grade II listed building.

At the Southern end of Salisbury Square is Marychurch. The church is connected to older buildings that previously formed the Church of the Blessed Sacrament and St Teresa (of Avila).

St Teresa's was opened in 1930 to the north of a row of terraces, in an area called Batterdale. This church was able to seat about 120 people. By the 1960s a growing congregation needed more space, and land to the south of the existing church was made available following the widening of the old Great North Road. Marychurch was built. The former church is now used for church activities, social events, and it becomes a polling station for local and national elections.

Marychurch was designed by George Mathers and built in 1970 by the building firm George Davis and Sons. The church has a round exterior circled by wide, brown-brick piers. Between the piers are tall, coloured-glass windows running the full height of the brickwork. The conical church roof supports an aluminium spire.

The coloured glass windows in Marychurch were designed by Charles Norris, a monk, trained at the Royal College of Art. He had previously worked with Paulinas Angold to develop the glass work at Buckfast Abbey. The windows are made using the "dalle de verre" technique developed in France in the 1920s.

The stained-glass panels to the north and south of the chapel, represent, respectively, a beam of light and the Tree of Jesse. The panels in the upper part contain images of the four evangelists, and the north wall features a dramatic scene of the Creation and the cosmos.

The crew of the Hatfield Fire service, formerly based in what is now Batterdale.

(6) THE FORMER SITE OF THE HOME AND BUSINESS OF THE BURGESS FAMILY

Walking away from Marychurch westwards towards French Horn Lane there is a subway that passes under A1000. On the far side of the underpass a plaque marks the site that was the former home and business premises of the Burgess Family. Batterdale was demolished following the re-development of Salisbury Square.

The plaque reads; "Beehive Makers, Builders, Bark and Timber Dealers, Clock Makers, Funeral Directors, and Monument Masons, birth place to what would later become the Merryweather Fire Engine and the domestic Bean Slice, both invented by James John Burgess".

(7) THE SALISBURY ARMS

The Salisbury Arms, formerly a hotel and restaurant, has distinctive chimneys.

The Salisbury Arms was commissioned by the Marquess of Salisbury in 1885 as a Temperance Hotel and was known locally as the 'Coffee Tavern'. The building has distinctive brick, Tudor-style, chimneys.

The building originally housed the Public Hall with a meeting room on the first floor capable of accommodating about 400 people. Later it became a restaurant, closing in the 1970s. The building is now used as offices.

To the left of the Old Salisbury restaurant is a barbers shop that was previously a jail house. The short stretch of road leading up to it was known as Cage Hill.

Over the road from the Salisbury Arms was another pub called the Dray Horse and the site of the old Market place. The site is now a small car park opposite Marychurch.

The Dray Horse and the Salisbury Arms hotel.

Bus 155 departing from the Dray Horse pub.

Broadway from Church Street towards the Eight Bells

The Broadway today.

(8) CHURCH STREET

Church Street, formerly Back Street, connects the two churches. It has a number of listed buildings.

For many years the street was called Back Street. It was renamed Church street in 1931.

Church Street has many old houses presenting differing styles and building methods. Many of the houses were built by the Gascoyne Cecil estate but are now in private ownership.

The houses on the right of the street have interesting brickwork, where bricks are used front and side on, sometimes called rat trap bond.

At the bend of the street is a house called the Traveller's Rest. This house was at one time a baker's house and shop. In the 1840s it became a tavern and lodging house and adopted its current name It closed as an inn in 1906. In the early 1920s it was bought and converted back to a house by F W Speaight.

(9) JACOB'S LADDER

Jacobs Ladder - This flight of steps leads from the original Salisbury square to Church street.

Halfway up Church Street is a flight of steps that lead down to what is now a car park.

The hollow at the base of the steps had previously been the old Workhouse Yard. In the 1850s a row of terraced cottages was built by the 2nd marquess of Salisbury for the staff of the Hertfordshire Militia. The area became known as Salisbury Square.

The area at the base of the steps became a garage for many years that faced onto London road, (Now the Broadway). In 1972 both the garage and the cottages were demolished and replaced by flats and offices.

(10) ST AUDREYS

St. Audrey's, built in 1889 on the original site of the Two Brewers alehouse. It is now a nursing home.

St Audrey's was built for the Reverend Lord William Gascoyne-Cecil, son of the 3rd Marquess of Salisbury in 1889, soon after his appointment as Rector. It had previously been the site of the Two Brewers alehouse.

In recent times St Audrey's has been a home for the blind and is now a nursing home.

(11) NO. 5 CHURCH STREET

No. 5 Church Street, built in 1853, this was originally a gate house to the Hatfield Park estate

At the top of Church street is the former gatehouse, now No. 5 Church Street. It was built on behalf the 2nd Marquess of Salisbury by the Estate's bricklayers in 1853. The house has an unusual style of random brickwork, possibly using bricks from the house that previously stood on the site.

The house was originally known as Back Street Lodge and controlled a gate across Church Street (Back St.). The gate was moved to the top of Church Street in 1881.

(12) ST ETHELDREDA'S CHURCH HALL

St Etheldreda's Church Hall. The building was originally Countess Anne's School.

St Etheldreda's Church Hall was built by the 3rd Marquess of Salisbury in 1869. The Tudor style building is built from red brick, with tiled roof and gable ends. It is entered through a porch. The brickwork surrounding the doors and windows copies the style of the Old Palace.

The hall was built to house the charity school set up by Anne, Countess of Salisbury, in 1732. In 1912 it became a Church of England Infant and Junior school but continued to bear the name of Countess Anne. Countess Anne school moved to a more central site in Hatfield town in 1962.

The building was subsequently converted for use as a church hall and was opened by Lord Salisbury in 1965. In 2017 the lease was handed back to the Gascoyne-Cecil Estate. They plan to make further alterations to the building.

(13) CHURCH COTTAGE AND THE BAKERS ARMS

Church Cottage, a timber-framed building dating from the 16th century.

At the entrance to the church yard we find the Baker's Arms. Originally a combined baker's shop and ale house. It was run by the Bradshaw family in the 1850s. It came into the ownership of Pryor Reid's Hatfield Brewery and continued as a licensed house until 1928.

Connected to the Bakers Arms is Church Cottage. Church Cottage is a 16th century timber-framed building, restored in 1920, and converted into cottages. For many years Church Cottage was the residence of the curates of the parish church.

(14) THE PARISH CHURCH OF ST ETHELDREDA

St Etheldreda's church dates from the 13th century. It is the parish church of Hatfield.

The earliest parts of St Etheldreda's church, the transepts date from 13th century. Since then the building has developed, with various sections being added to form the church we see today. The Brocket Chapel, to the south, and the tower were added in the 15th century. The Salisbury Chapel, to the north, was built in 1618. The church was heavily restored in 1871 by the 3rd Marquess of Salisbury and the nave was completely rebuilt. The architect was David Brandon.

The tower has four stages and has been topped by various spires and spikes over the centuries. The last, a shingled spire, was erected in 1847 to commemorate Queen Victoria's visit to Hatfield. It was dismantled in 1930.

The graveyard has an interesting collection of tombstones. John Whitemore's grave is a memorial to a man reputed to have lived in three centuries. Born in 1698 he died in 1801 at the age of 103. The grave of Fanny Twelvetrees lies at the end of 12 yew trees in the far corner of the grounds.

(15) INSIDE ST ETHELDREDA'S CHURCH

St Etheldreda's church contains the tomb of Robert Cecil and several remarkable stained-glass windows.

The church is built on a traditional cruciform plan with North and South porches extending from the nave. The tower is at the west, with two side chapels at the opposite end.

The Salisbury Chapel, to the north, was built it 1618. It was designed by Francis Carter for William, 2nd Earl of Salisbury, as mortuary chapel for his father. The interior was redecorated in 1871 by the 3rd Marquess of Salisbury who added mosaic walls, a painted panelled ceiling and wrought iron gates.

The central monument honours Robert Cecil, 1st Earl of Salisbury (d. 1612) it was made by the King's sculptor, Maximilian

Colt. The chapel also features the tomb of a 13th century knight, and an effigy of William Curll by Nicholas Stone, dating from 1617.

The Brocket Chapel, to the South, was Built in the 15th century. It was originally the private chapel of the Fortescue family and it contains the tombs of the later Brockets and Reades of Brocket Hall. The chapel features a large marble standing monument to Sir James Reade designed by Michael Rysbrack in 1765, a wall mounted plaque commemorating Sir John Brocket dating from 1598, and the tomb of 2nd Viscount Melbourne (d.1848).

The tower contains ten bells. It also contains a carillon, originally housed in St Peter's Church, St Albans. It was given to the parish by Emily Mary, First Marchioness of Salisbury in 1805. When working, it plays daily at 9.00am, noon, 3.00pm and 6.00pm with a different peal for each day of the week.

Records from 1610 state there were originally there were five large bells, plus a Sanctus bell, in the tower. In the 17th century the pub at the bottom of Fore Street was similarly called the Five Bells. In 1739 three new bells were added and the pub's name was changed to the Eight Bells.

In 1929, two further bells were added in memory of Rupert Edward Gascoyne-Cecil who was killed at Ypres in 1915. These, combined with the original eight bells brought the total up to ten. However, the pub's name remained unchanged.

The church has some interesting stained-glass windows. The window in the south transept was designed by Edward Burne-Jones in 1894. The Cecil memorial window, in the middle of the nave, was commissioned by the Fourth Marquess of Salisbury in 1920, to commemorate his three nephews who had been killed in the first World War 1914-18. The window features three angel figures symbolising Trial and Sacrifice, Victory and Triumph, and The Guardian Angel. It was designed by Christopher Whall.

(16) SALISBURY BURIAL GROUND

The Salisbury burial ground lies in an area between St Etheldreda's church and the Old Palace.

The Salisbury cemetry is located to the North of the church between St Etheldreda's and the Old Palace. It was constructed on what had previously been part of the main road from London to the North until the road was diverted at the time of the construction of the railway through Hatfield in 1850.

In the centre of the burial ground for the Cecil family is a cross dating from 1872. It is surrounded by the graves of the Gascoyne-Cecil family members and some of their pets.

(17) REAL TENNIS COURT

The real tennis court at Hatfield House was built in 1842. It has been an independent club since 1955.

The real tennis court at Hatfield House was built in 1842 by the 2nd Marquess of Salisbury. Following its completion, the Cecils and their guests used this court exclusively for nearly 100 years until the outbreak of war in 1939. The court was used as a store throughout the war and for several years afterwards. In 1955 the 5th Marquess allowed a number of local players to reopen it and form a private club.

Real tennis is the predecessor of modern court-based racquet sports. The game is played, over a net, but it is played indoors on a closed court. The walls of the court form part of the playing area, as well as the roofs of galleries built into three sides. The court resembles monastery cloisters and is asymmetric. The scoring system allows players to score points depending on where the ball hits objects marked on the side of the court.

In the late 1860s, Lord Salisbury wished to play real tennis on his court at Hatfield House. However, Lady Salisbury had already booked the court. Charles Lambert, the real tennis professional at Hatfield House, was instructed to make up an alternative game suitable for Lady Salisbury and her friends.

Consequently, Charles, with his brother, George, devised a game of "lawn" tennis for the ladies to play. They hooked up a real tennis net on the lawn, provided rackets and balls, devised rules. This event was not the first lawn tennis. However, it may have had some impact on the modern game.

Charles and George Lambert's initiative was followed by lawn tennis being played outside the real tennis court at Lord's and the setting up a Lawn Tennis Sub-Committee to form rules of the game. When the rules of lawn tennis were formally instituted for the Wimbledon Championship in 1877, they included the traditional real tennis scoring of 15, 30, 40 and game - based on a clock's 4 quarter hours.

In the courtyard we can also find the Old Palace.

(18) THE OLD PALACE

The Old Palace was built in about 1479. Formerly the childhood home of Elizabeth I, it is now used as a banqueting hall and for other functions.

The original building was built in 1479 by Cardinal Morton the Bishop of Ely. It is a very good example of early brick construction and was originally built as a quadrangle. Three sides of the original palace were pulled down when new House was built.

The palace was acquired by King Henry VIII from the Bishop of Ely in 1538. The King then used it as a nursery for his three children, including Elizabeth.

Henry's daughter Mary came to the throne in 1553. Fearing that her enemies might plot to place her protestant sister on the throne, she ordered that Elizabeth be confined to Hatfield.

Queen Mary died in 1558. She left no heirs. Elizabeth became queen. Tradition has it that she was given the news when she was sitting by an oak tree in the park. This tree became known as Queen Elizabeth Oak.

One of Elizabeth's first acts upon her succession to the throne was to call together her trusted advisers for her first Council of State. The meeting was held in the Banqueting Hall of what is now called the Old Palace.

In 1607 King James I exchanged the Palace at Hatfield for Theobalds, the home of Robert Cecil, 1st Earl of Salisbury. Robert Cecil then embarked on building Hatfield House on the site. This involved demolishing three-quarters of the original manor house.

What is now the Old Palace is the one side of the original bishop's palace. The building was used as stables for the next three centuries, until it was restored to its present use by the 4th Marquess in 1915.

The palace was used as a hospital during the first world war, when beds were installed to look after wounded soldiers. The building is now used for weddings and other functions.

(19) STABLE YARD IN HATFIELD PARK

Stable Yard became a retail area in 2010. At the centre is a fountain featuring a pineapple.

The original buildings around Stable Yard were built in 1915. At the same time the Old Palace was restored for use as a banqueting hall. This became the stabling area, changing over time to garage vehicles as the car replaced horses as the main means of travel.

In 2010 the area was transformed into a courtyard of shops and a restaurant. In the centre there is a fountain. In the middle of the fountain a white obelisk supports a sculpted stone pineapple, the traditional symbol of hospitality.

(20) THE OLD SALISBURY ARMS

The old Salisbury Arms or White Lion was a coaching inn.

The old Salisbury Arms is next to the Hatfield Park lodge at the top of Fore Street.

From the early 17th century until 1881 the old Salisbury Arms or White Lion was an important coaching inn. It became a regular stop for coaches travelling between London and the North as it lay on the route of the road to London that travelled up Fore Street and passed by what is now called the Old Palace.

The present building dates from the mid-1700s. It features an archway that led to a yard providing stabling for up to 40 horses, this archway is now bricked up. There are also some blocked-up windows. This is commonly supposed to be a legacy of the Window Tax which was payable from 1696 until 1851. However, as the tax already applicable when the building was erected, it is more likely attributable to design rather than having windows removed for tax management.

(21) EAST INDIA HOUSE

East India House (10 Fore Street) dates from the early 18th century. The building was formerly a tavern called, the East Indian Chief.

East India House opened as a public house in the mid-18th century, taking advantage, of its position adjacent to the market place. It became known as the Marquess of Granby and was later called the Full Measure. By 1855 it had become the East Indian Chief. It was closed around 1960 when it was once more converted to private use.

The market house stood in the courtyard opposite the pub from the mid-18th century for almost 100 years when it was demolished and relocated to the base of Fore Street. The Market House was a covered trading area, with open space on the lower level for all weather trading.

Fore Street and the East India Chief around 1915.

Fore street decorated for a royal event.

(22) FORE STREET

Fore Street, formerly part of the main route between London and the North, still has many old buildings reflecting its past.

One of the early routes between London and the North took traffic down Fore Street. The road became known as London Road. It became a popular rest stop on the route many trades and hostelries grew up along the road.

The Rectory, stands adjacent to the gates of St. Etheldreda's church. The present house was built around 1600 by Fulk Onslow, Clerk of the Parliaments to Queen Elizabeth. It became the official Rectory when it was donated to the diocese by Lord Salisbury in 1954.

Garden House (16 Fore Street) was the residence of a succession of surgeons and apothecaries in the 18th century. By the mid-19th century it had become a boarding school run by Thomas Ray, a non-conformist clergyman.

Thomas Hardy spent a few weeks here as a day-pupil, in the

summer of 1849 the while staying with his uncle in the town. He was not enthusiastic about his experience.

On the left side on the way down the hill, 11 Fore Street was previously a Butchers shop and still has hooks over the doorway. It is now a private house.

The street had several pubs and inns. The Rose and Crown was located at 40-42 Fore street, becoming the town's telephone exchange in 1904.

The King's Head Inn was located at 21-25 Fore Street. This large, early 18th century building was one of the four inns that then faced onto the market place located at the lower end of Fore Street. By 1838 it had been converted into shops and was used as the town post office from the middle of the century until 1885. It is now used as offices.

Fore street around 1900.

(23) THE EIGHT BELLS

The Eight Bells has been an inn since the 17th century. it is associated with Charles Dickens in Oliver Twist.

The Eight Bells is a 17th century building. It was first recorded as an inn when it was acquired by John Searancke, in 1728. In 1756 it was licensed to Andrew Harrow and listed as having three bedrooms and stabling for four horses.

It is probably best known as the inn associated with Charles Dickens' novel Oliver Twist. It is the pub visited by Bill Sikes after the murder of Nancy. Charles Dickens visited Hatfield as a newspaper reporter in 1835 after a fire at Hatfield House which caused the death of the Dowager Lady Salisbury.

The premises were refurbished in the 1960s when they were expanded into the adjoining shop.

The Eight Bells

Workers at the Pryor Reid Brewery, located in Brewery Hill, now Salisbury Square.

(24) CHEQUERS

Site of the original Chequers Inn. In the 1660. the "Hatfield Token Half Penny" was issued from here.

The Chequers Inn stood on this site from the 15th century. In the 1800s it was converted into a brewery. The brewery was connected to the Eight Bells by connecting tunnels. In the 1950s it was a Haberdashers and more recently has become offices.

In the 1660s. the "Hatfield Token Half Penny" was issued by the then landlord, Thomas Serin or Searancke. The coin is an example of a trade token. These were issued due to a shortage of official coins, particularly lower values. Tokens were widely issued by tradesmen and innkeepers. However, these tokens could generally only be used in the shop or business that issued them.

Next to Chequers is the Old Coach House dating from around 1500. Bakers traded from these premises from the mid-18th century until the 1940s. It is now a private residence.

(25) PARK CLOSE THE SITE OF THE PARK STREET CHAPEL

The site of Park Street Chapel until 1932. Headstones from the graveyard remain along the wall at the top of the Close.

Hatfield "Park Street Chapel"

Park Street is the site of the Park Street Chapel, the first non-conformist place of worship in Hatfield, built in 1823. The building was demolished in 1932. The headstones from the graveyard were re located and may be seen along the wall at the top of Park Close.

Formerly called Duck Lane, Park Street had a variety of shops including basket makers, bakers, and Walby the butcher. Walby was a family business that remained in Hatfield from the 1780s until the 1970s.

Park Street around 1900.

Walby the butcher on Park Street, around 1920.

(26) THE HORSE AND GROOM PUB

The Horse and Groom pub dates back to 1806.

The Horse and Groom has been a pub since 1806. It has a low-timbered interior including a snug around the old fireplace.

The small alley to the right of the pub is the route of the former Arm and Sword lane.

Park Street and the Horse and Groom in the 1900s

(27) ARM AND SWORD LANE

Arm and Sword lane, also known as Blood and Guts Alley, due to the nearby slaughter house.

The former Arm and Sword lane is a narrow cutting that formerly led directly from Park Street to the Great North Road. It was originally adjacent to the Arm and Sword Inn (possibly an earlier name of the Horse and Groom). Until the early years of this century it was lined on both sides with small cottages. It was known as Blood and Guts Alley or Bug Alley due to the butchers and slaughterhouse that were located nearby.

In 1901 Henry Walby and his brother James had a butcher's shop on the corner of Park Street and Arm and Sword Yard. Other residents of the yard included brickmakers, railway workers, carpenters, laundresses and straw plaiters. In 2015 a new Arm and Sword Lane was re-instated as part of the Old Hatfield regeneration. It stands about 50 metres from the originally named street.

(28) HILL HOUSE

Hill House is a Georgian residence. Once the home of Seymour Clarke, the first General Manager of the Great Northern Railway.

This imposing late Georgian residence was built by a member of the Hall family, well-established local builders and landowners at the time. In the mid-19th century the house was occupied by Seymour Clarke, the first General Manager of the Great Northern Railway. The house was bought by the Gascoyne-Cecil Estate in the 1940s and in 1958 was converted into flats.

(29) HATFIELD VIADUCT

Hatfield Viaduct, built in 1877 to provide access from Hatfield House to the railway station for the 3rd Marquess of Salisbury.

The Hatfield Viaduct was built to connect Hatfield House to Hatfield Railway station. Commissioned by the 3rd Marquess of Salisbury, it was completed in 1877 by Gentle, builders of St Albans.

The view from Hatfield Viaduct around 1920.

The view from Hatfield Viaduct 2017.

(30) THE A1000 AND PARK MEADOW

Following the path along Park Street, the route takes us behind Park Meadow to the Old Hertford Road.

Park Meadow was built in the 1960s on land belonging to the Gascoyne-Cecil estates. On the right is the outer edge of Hatfield Park. Park Street leads into the Old Hertford Road, where we can see a few of the older houses that predate the Park Meadow development.

The Old Hertford road was once the main road connecting Hatfield and Hertford. However, the road was re-routed in 1894, creating the current cross roads at the traffic lights next to the Red Lion. The far end of the road was later closed off.

At the upper end of the road we arrive at the Red Lion.

(31) THE RED LION

The Red Lion dates back to the late 18th century it is located at the junction of the main routes through the town.

The main road, the Great North Road originally ran past the South side of the building. It was re-routed to the north side of the site since 1864. In 1894 the road from Hertford to St Albans was diverted a few yards further north with the construction of the new railway bridge

During the 19th century a livestock and corn market was held on the land to the north of the inn. The land became a car park, and was converted to flats in the 1990s. The original Red Lion lamp post is still situated within the new development.

The Red Lion around 1900.

Soldiers returning to Hatfield marching past the Salisbury hotel along the former London Road after the first world war (1921).

(32) NORTH PLACE

North Place is a substantial residence that can be traced back to 1705, in recent years it has been used as offices.

North Place dates from 1705. It was occupied for much of the 18th century by a succession of curates. In the 1780s the young William Lamb, later to become Queen Victoria's first Prime Minister, boarded for a few years with his tutor, the Rev Thomas Marsham.

The house, which was enlarged in the late 19th century, has for many years been used as offices. It is now run as the Great North Business centre, offering short term office space leasing.

(33) HATFIELD SOCIAL CLUB

Hatfield Social Club was built on the current site in 1970. It replaced the former home of the Home Guard.

Hatfield Social club was established in 1934. It originally ran from a premises a few hundred metres from the present site donated by Lord Salisbury.

The club moved to its present location in 1970 following the restructure of Salisbury Square and the re-routing of the A1000. The new clubhouse replaced the former headquarters of the Home Guard, that previously stood on the site.

(34) MARQUIS HOUSE

Marquis House on the A1000 was formerly the General Post Office telephone exchange and is now used as offices.

Marquis House on the A1000 was built in 1936 as the main Post Office and telephone exchange for Hatfield. Outside the building are two original wrought iron lamp posts, without their lamps. The building was opened on May 25th 1936 by the 4th Marquess of Salisbury. A carved stone plaque commemorates this event.

(35) THE HATFIELD WAR MEMORIAL

The Hatfield War Memorial commemorates local men and women lost during the First and Second World Wars.

The War Memorial Garden was officially opened on 12th June 1921 by Lord Hampden, The Lord Lieutenant of Hertfordshire. The dedication ceremony was conducted by the Bishop of Exeter who, while Rector at Hatfield, had lost three sons in the War. The pavilion displays the names of those who died in the World Wars, commemorating 141 local men lost during the First World War and a further 92 killed in the Second World War.

The central cross features roses and lilies representing England and France. It stands in the centre of the lawn. Two memorial cast iron benches were also added to the garden.

The Hatfield War Memorial is one of 24 war memorials in England designed by Sir Herbert Baker. He is one of the architects of New Delhi. It was listed by Historic England in 2017.

APPENDIX

The Appendix includes some additional sites in vicinity of Old Hatfield. The two memorials can be found following a short walk down the A1000.

(A) HATFIELD PARK WAR MEMORIAL

The Hatfield Park War Memorial is located about 400 metres from the roundabout along the A1000. The entrance consists of a wooden gate leading to a set of steps which in turn lead up to the cemetery. Care should be taken crossing the road and parking here is dangerous.

During the Second World War Hatfield House was used as a military hospital. After the war a small section of the Park was enclosed and laid out as a cemetery for burials from this hospital.

Hatfield Park War Cemetery contains 20 graves together with that of a civilian airman (a flight test observer, who died in 1943).

(B) HATFIELD TRAIN CRASH MEMORIAL

A small wood panelled memorial garden commemorates the victims of the Hatfield rail crash accident on 17 October 2000.

The memorial is located about 800 metres along the A1000 from the Old Hatfield roundabout. Again care should be taken crossing the road and parking would be dangerous.

(C) MILL GREEN MILL AND MUSEUM

Located just under a mile from Hatfield station is Mill Green. The small hamlet includes a working watermill and museum set in an attractive riverside setting. The watermill dates from the eighteenth century.

The Old Hatfield Trail

A postcard of Old Hatfield. Produced in 2017 from pictures taken by residents.

Available from;

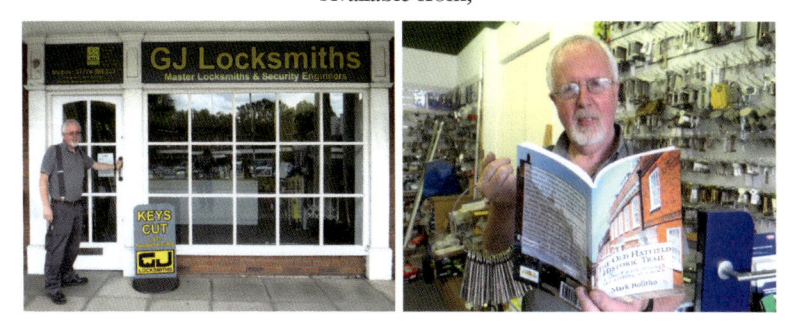

GJ Locksmiths, 9 The Broadway. www.g-j-locksmiths.co.uk
The Horse and Groom and the Eight Bells.

Mark Bolitho

Can you find these places in Old Hatfield ?

1 _____

2 _____

3 _____

4 _____

The Old Hatfield Trail

5 _____

6 _____

7 _____

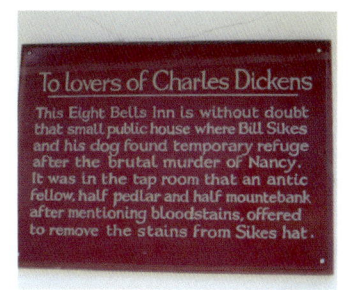

> To lovers of Charles Dickens
>
> This Eight Bells Inn is without doubt that small public house where Bill Sikes and his dog found temporary refuge after the brutal murder of Nancy. It was in the tap room that an antic fellow, half pedlar and half mountebank after mentioning bloodstains, offered to remove the stains from Sikes hat.

8 _____

Salisbury

SERO SED SERIO

9 _____

10 _____

63

Mark Bolitho

11

12

13

14

15

16

The Old Hatfield Trail

17 _____

18 _____

19 _____

20 _____

21 _____

22 _____

ANSWERS

1) The pineapple, symbol of hospitality. Stable Yard.
2) Marychurch.
3) The gates of Hatfield House.
4) The Red Lion pub sign, Great North Road.
5) Door knocker on the Broadway
6) The gates to the war memorial.
7) The eight bells pub.
8) The Salisbury Arms hotel.
9) A man hole outside Marquis House.
10) A torch holder at the gate house of Hatfield House.
11) The underpass beneath the A1000.
12) Entrance to St Ethedreda's Church Tower.
13) A painted window at the top of Fore Street.
14) Post box at the top of Fore Street.
15) St Etheldreda's Church clock
16) St Etheldreda's Church
17) Chimneys on the Salisbury Hotel
18) Marychurch bell tower
19) Marquis House.
20) The Salisbury cemetery gates.
21) The War memorial garden.
22) A light outside the Great Northern.

The Old Hatfield Trail

The "Beauties" of Hatfield cannot be exaggerated. Too busy to write.

Mark Bolitho

Thanks to supporters of the project, including Brian Lawrence, Chris Goward, Margaret Stephens, Simon Bolitho, Constance Elliot, Jonathan Fisher, James Wilding, the team at the Hatfield House Archive, The Old Hatfield Residents Association, and Hatfield Library.

Printed in Great Britain
by Amazon